Primer Level / Level One
(Prep / Grade 1)

CLASSIC MELODIES from
GREAT SYMPHONIES

For Piano
for beginners of all ages

compiled and arranged by
John W. Schaum

New Editing and Revised Arrangements by Wesley Schaum

Foreword

This series helps develop music appreciation early in a student's piano study. The books are appropriate for adults and children. Very easy arrangements enable the student to play famous melodies by the world's great composers.

Duet accompaniments are included for each melody. The ensemble experience provides valuable rhythmic training and makes the music sound more complete.

In this book of *Great Symphonies*, the best known name is used for the title of each symphony. The year of completion is shown with each title. The book sequence is in chronological order of the composers' birth dates.

Other albums in this series are:

- Classic Melodies from GREAT BALLETS
  Themes, illustrations and stories from 20 famous ballets
- Classic Melodies from GREAT COMPOSERS
  Famous themes by 20 master composers from Bach to Bartok
- Classic Melodies from GREAT OPERAS
  Includes Aida, Carmen, La Boheme, Madame Butterfly, Pagliacci

SCHAUM PUBLICATIONS, INC.
10235 N. Port Washington Rd. • Mequon, WI • 53092

Music Notation by Jeff Schaum and Wesley Schaum

07-44
N-14

Typical Seating Plan of a Symphony Orchestra

Many symphony orchestras of today consist of nearly one hundred players.

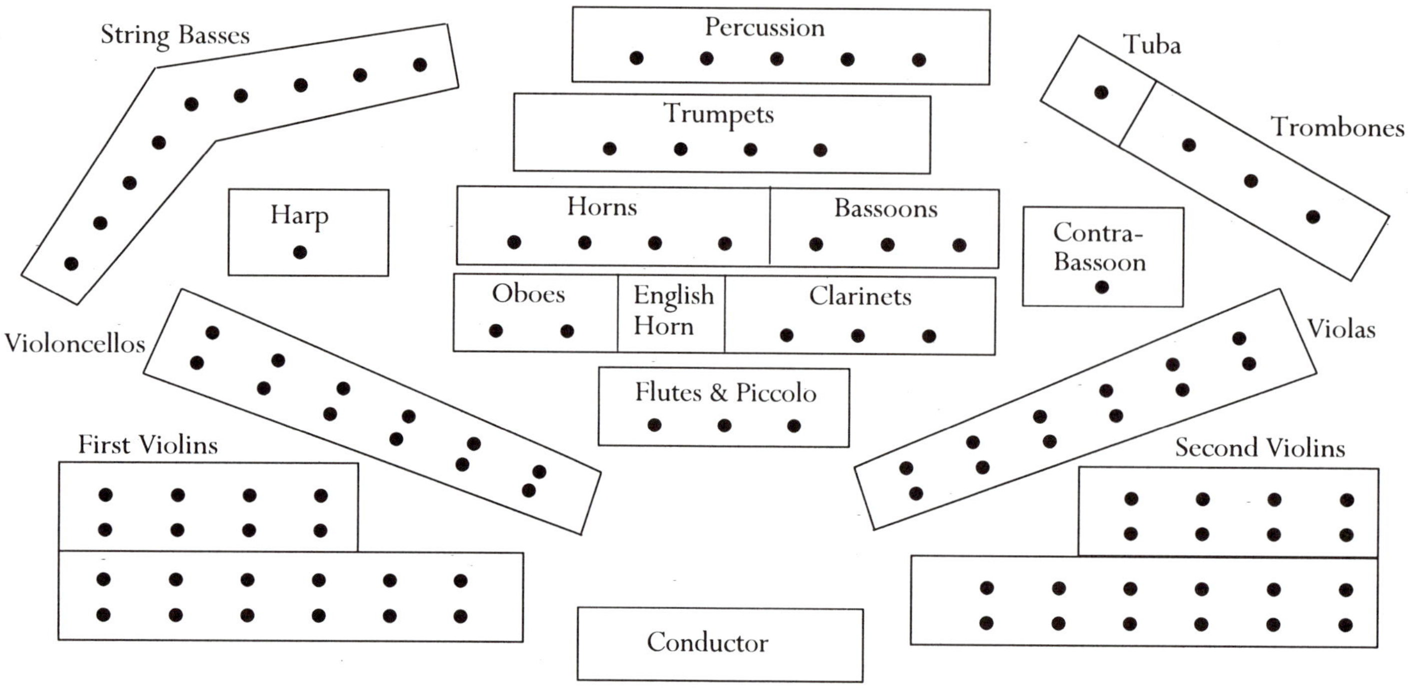

Composer Index

The Schaum Music Memory Game "Great Symphonies" – page 24

String Family

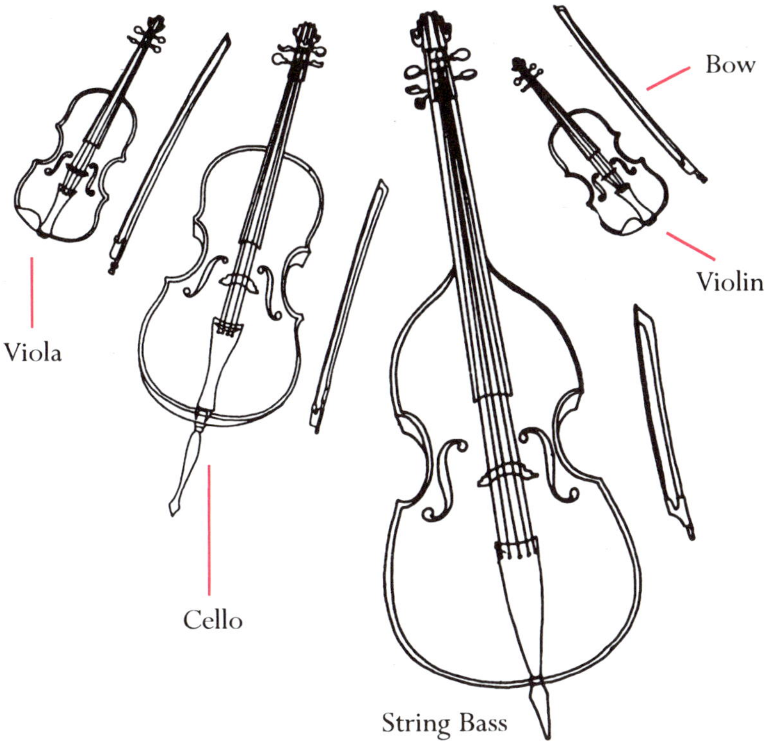

The size of each instrument is proportionally correct within each family.

The *larger* the instrument, the *lower* the sound it can produce.

The piano can sound lower and higher than any of the instruments shown here.

Woodwind Family

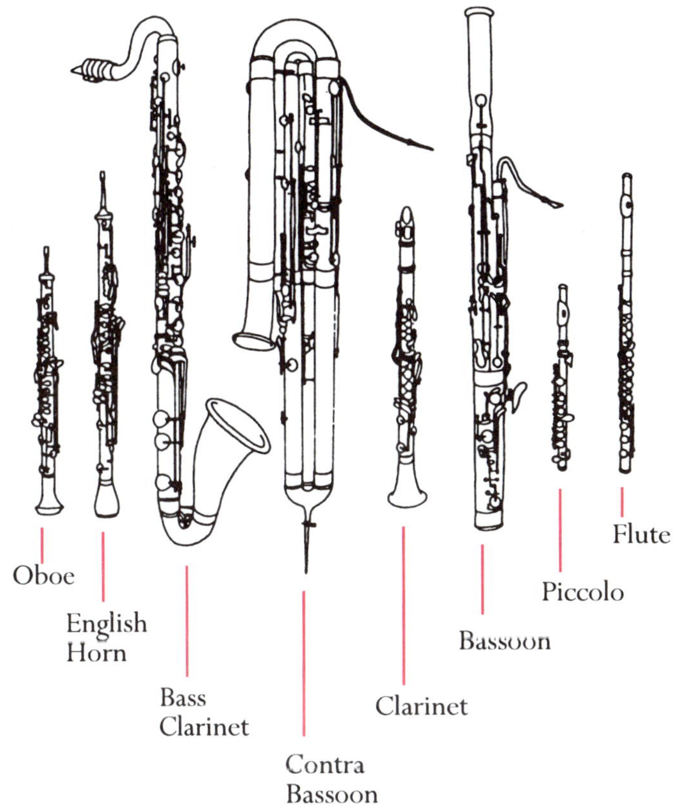

Brass Family

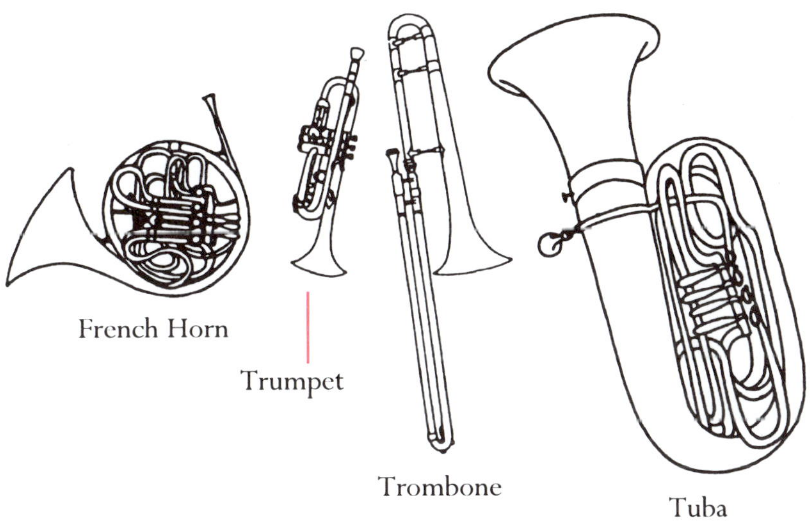

Percussion Family

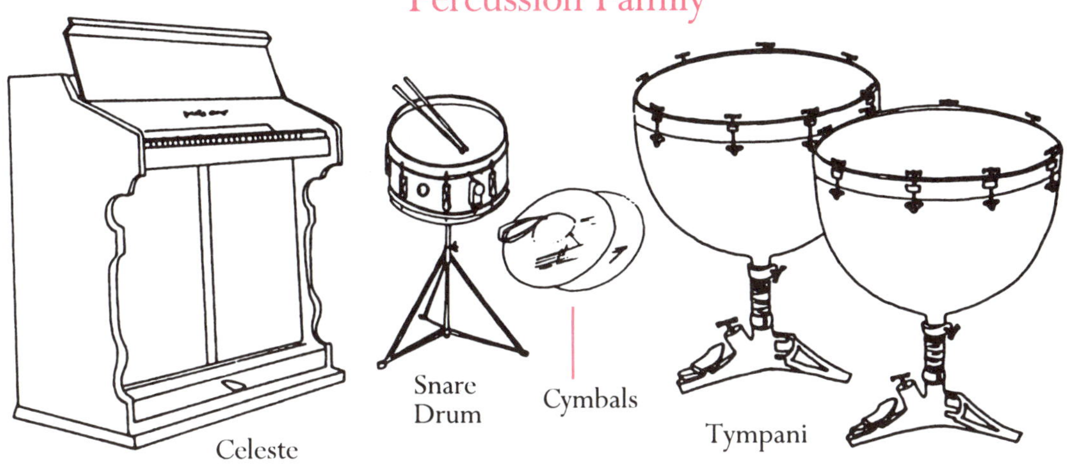

Haydn (1732-1809)

"Surprise" Symphony No. 94 (1791)

Theme from 2nd Movement

A symphony is an elaborate composition for orchestra consisting of a group of three or four parts (movements), each in a different style.

Franz Joseph Haydn is known as the father of the symphony and was nicknamed "Papa Haydn." In his famous "Surprise Symphony" he suddenly injected a loud chord to surprise and awaken certain inattentive listeners.

place
Violin stamp
here

Duet Accompaniment

Haydn (1732-1809)

"Clock" Symphony No.101 (1794)

Theme from 2nd Movement

The largest section of the symphony orchestra is the string family which consists of the violin, viola, cello (violoncello) and string bass (double bass).

In stringed instruments, the sound comes from vibrating strings. Pulling a bow across the strings makes the vibrations. Occasionally the strings are plucked by hand for staccato effects such as in this melody from the "Clock Symphony." In his lifetime Haydn wrote 125 symphonies.

place Viola stamp here

Duet Accompaniment

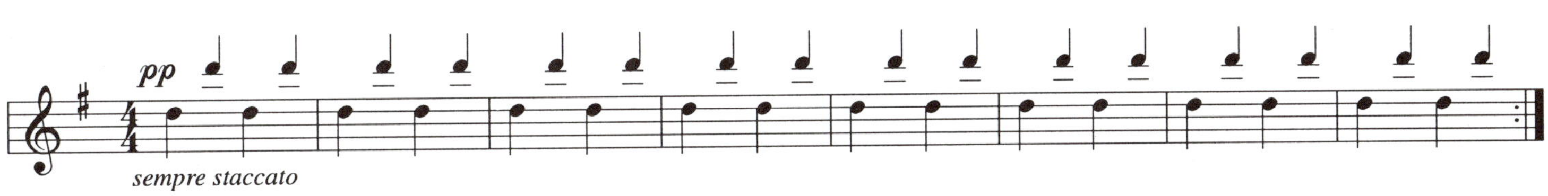

Haydn (1732-1809)

"Farewell" Symphony No. 45 (1772)

Theme from 4th Movement

Haydn's "Farewell" or "Candle Symphony" has a clever touch of humor. In the final movement of the symphony, the musicians leave one by one, each blowing out the candle on his music stand as he departs, until only two violinists are left. At the close they blow out their candles and leave.

This was Haydn's subtle way of suggesting that he and his musicians needed a vacation. Their patron, Prince Esterhazy, graciously took the hint and granted them a leave of absence.

place
Cello stamp
here

Duet Accompaniment

Mozart (1756-1791)

Symphony No. 39 K543 (1788)

Theme from 3rd Movement

Ludwig von Köchel (KESH-el) was an admirer of Mozart. Köchel compiled a descriptive catalog of all of Mozart's music, listed in chronological order. In Köchel's catalog, the code number K543 means it was the 543rd composition written by Mozart.

This enormous task was not started until 60 years after Mozart's death. Köchel carefully studied all of Mozart's manuscripts, taking eleven years to complete the catalog.

place
String Bass
stamp here

Tempo di Minuet

Duet Accompaniment

Mozart (1756-1791)

Symphony No. 40 K550 (1788)

Theme from 1st Movement

The orchestras that Mozart conducted were smaller than today's symphony orchestras. At the time of both Haydn and Mozart, the orchestras had about 42 players consisting of:

- 8 first violins
- 8 second violins
- 5 violas
- 5 cellos
- 4 string basses
- 2 flutes
- 2 clarinets (occasionally)
- 2 oboes (occasionally)
- 2 horns
- 2 trumpets
- 2 kettledurms

(Sometimes there were only 4 to 6 wind instruments.)

place
Flute stamp
here

Duet Accompaniment

Mozart (1756-1791)

"Jupiter" Symphony No. 41, K551 (1788)

Theme from 3rd Movement

The last three of Mozart's symphonies, Nos. 39, 40 and 41, are his most popular. All three were written during the same year, 1788. J.B. Cramer, a famous music critic, added the nickname "Jupiter" because of the "loftiness and nobility of the music."

The woodwind family is so named because these instruments were originally made from wooden tubes. They include the flute, piccolo, clarinet, bass clarinet, oboe, English horn, bassoon and contrabassoon. The modern flute and piccolo are usually made of a metal tube, sometimes silver or gold. The other instruments may be made of plastic tubes, but wood is usually preferred for better sound quality.

place
Piccolo stamp
here

Duet Accompaniment

Beethoven (1770-1827)

"Eroica" Symphony No. 3, Op. 55 (1804)

Theme from 2nd Movement

When he wrote this symphony in 1804, Beethoven intended to honor Napoleon Bonaparte, the famous French leader. "Eroica" means heroic. The music is said to portray the triumphs and eventual death of Napoleon. However, for reasons unknown, Beethoven never formally dedicated the symphony to Napoleon.

place
Clarinet stamp
here

Duet Accompaniment

Beethoven (1770-1827)

Fifth Symphony Op. 67 (1808)

Theme from 1st Movement

"Fate knocking at the door" is the description Beethoven gave to this symphony. However, during World War II it was called the "Victory" Symphony. At the time, the letter V was commonly used to symbolize victory. By coincidence, the telegraph code for the letter V (3 dots + a dash) is like the rhythm Beethoven used in the opening theme of this symphony!

place
Bass Clarinet
stamp here

Duet Accompaniment

Beethoven (1770-1827)

"Pastorale" Symphony No. 6, Op. 68 (1808)

Theme from 3rd Movement

Beethoven admired the wonders of nature and would take long leisurely walks in the country. His "Pastorale Symphony" reflects the composer's love of nature. The third movement represents a village festival with merry-making by the peasants.

The oboe is the instrument which sounds the tone A from which the entire orchestra tunes up.

place
Oboe stamp
here

Duet Accompaniment

Beethoven (1770-1827)

Seventh Symphony Op. 92 (1812)

Theme from 2nd Movement

Richard Wagner referred to this symphony as 'glorifying the dance.' Although the movements are not actual dance forms, the melodies are clear cut and rhythmical.

Beethoven increased the size of the orchestra by adding extra horns and enlarging the string section to about forty-five players, creating an orchestra of approximately sixty musicians.

place
English Horn
stamp here

Duet Accompaniment

Schubert (1797-1828)
"Unfinished" Symphony No. 8 (1822)

Theme from 1st Movement

Schubert wrote nine symphonies, including the "Unfinished," which is his best known. Most symphonies have three or four movements or sections. The "Unfinished," however, has only two movements. No one knows why it was not completed. 150 years after his death, sketches were found for a tenth symphony written by Schubert near the end of his life.

place
Bassoon stamp
here

Duet Accompaniment

Mendelssohn (1809-1847)

"Italian" Symphony No. 4, Op. 90 (1833)

Theme from 1st Movement

The most popular of Mendelssohn's four symphonies is the "Italian." It was inspired by the composer's trip to Italy in 1831. He completed it two years later and conducted it in concert with the Berlin Philharmonic Orchestra. It is obvious from the music that Mendelssohn enjoyed his trip to Italy very much.

place Contra-Bassoon stamp here

Duet Accompaniment

Schumann (1810-1856)

Fourth Symphony Op. 120 (1851)

Theme from 3rd Movement

This might be called the "Winter Symphony" since it is the last written by Schumann. The melody here is very robust and suggests a blustery winter wind.

The brass family of instruments consists of the trumpet, French horn, trombone and tuba. They are made from brass tubes of various sizes. The sound is produced by the player's lips vibrating in a cup-shaped mouthpiece.

place
Trumpet stamp
here

Duet Accompaniment

Franck (1822-1890)

Symphony in D Minor (1889)

Theme from 1st Movement

Cesar Franck wrote only one symphony but it ranks high in quality and popularity. Franck was born in Belgium, but spent most of his life in France where he became a professor at the Paris Conservatory and organist at the church of St. Clotilde.

The curved tubing in a French horn is necessary to make it compact and playable. Otherwise it would be a brass tube twelve feet long! This principle of compactness applies to all the brass instruments.

place
French horn
stamp here

Duet Accompaniment

Brahms (1833-1897)

First Symphony Op. 68 (1876)

Theme from 4th Movement

Many musicians consider the four symphonies of Brahms to be among the best ever written. He began composing his first symphony in 1855, but did not finish it until 21 years later. The First Symphony is probably his most popular.

Brahms had a flair for fun and humor. For example, he once said that his best ideas came to him as he polished his shoes in the morning.

place
Trombone stamp
here

Duet Accompaniment

Tchaikowsky (1840-1893)

Fourth Symphony Op. 36 (1878)

Theme from 2nd Movement

Tchaikowsky's fourth symphony is considered one of his best works. It was dedicated to his wealthy patroness, Mme. Von Meck. Her generous financial support extended over thirteen years.

During this time, Tchaikowsky wrote some of his greatest music. Curiously, the composer and his benefactress never met. They knew each other only by correspondence.

place
Tuba stamp
here

Duet Accompaniment

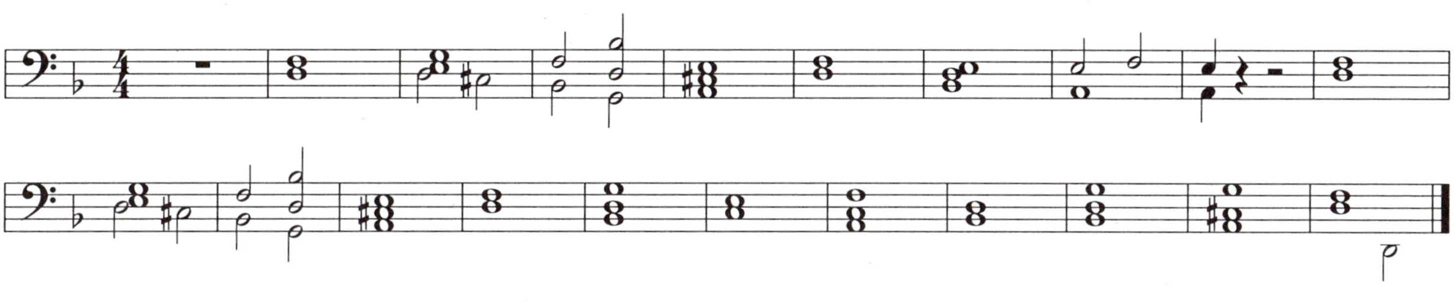

Tchaikowsky (1840-1893)

Fifth Symphony Op. 64 (1888)

Theme from 2nd Movement

Following Germany and Austria, Russia ranks third among the countries for outstanding symphonies. Tchaikowsky (chy-CUFF-skee) is unquestionably the most popular of all Russian composers. He wrote six symphonies, of which the last three are the great favorites.

Tchaikowsky had extravagant tastes in fashionable clothes and frequently spent more than his budget allowed.

place
Tympani stamp
here

Duet Accompaniment

Tchaikowsky (1840-1893)

"Pathetique" Symphony No. 6, Op. 74 (1893)

Theme from 1st Movement

Tchaikowsky's Sixth Symphony is called the "Pathetique" (pah-thuh-TEEK) because of the sombre mood of the music. This was the last piece of music he wrote. He died nine days after its first performance.

The percussion family of instruments consists of the tympani (kettledrums), bass drum, snare drum, chimes, gong, celeste and many smaller instruments including cymbals and triangle.

place
Percussion stamp
here

Duet Accompaniment

Dvorak (1841-1904)

"New World" Symphony No. 9, Op. 95 (1893)

Theme from 2nd Movement

Dvorak (DVOR-zhock) was born in Bohemia, now a part of the Czech Republic. He is the best known composer of that country.

In 1892 he visited the United States and stayed for three years. During that time he composed his Ninth Symphony. He gave it the title, "From the New World," because the music was influenced by his visit to America. This symphony was first performed in New York City.

place
Harp stamp
here

Duet Accompaniment

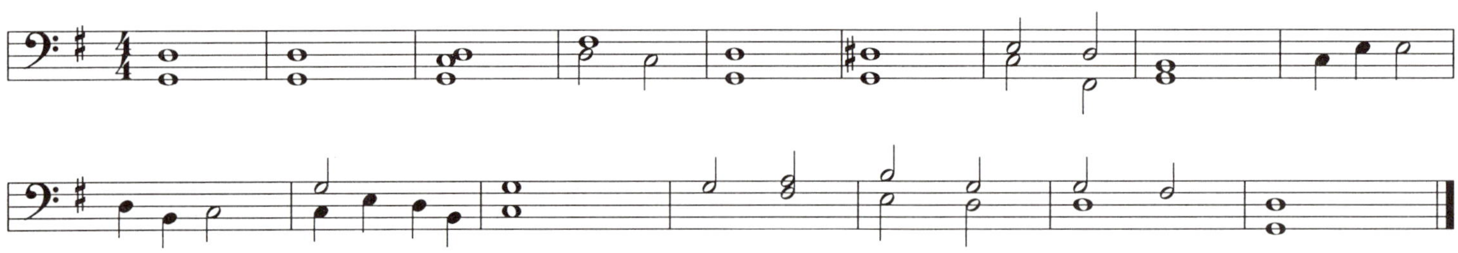

Mahler (1860-1911)

Fourth Symphony (1901)

Theme from 1st Movement

Mahler was an Austrian composer best known for his nine symphonies and vocal music. His symphonies are lengthy and require a very large orchestra. For example, the Fourth Symphony takes over 45 minutes to perform and includes a soprano soloist in the last movement. Each movement has numerous melodies, and uses instruments in unique combinations to produce dramatic effects.

For several years Mahler was conductor of the Metropolitan Opera orchestra in New York and of the New York Philharmonic orchestra.

place
Celeste stamp
here

Duet Accompaniment

The Schaum Music Memory Game

Directions: Below are four-measure themes from each of the twenty pieces in this book. They are out of order. Name each theme by looking at the list of titles and writing the correct number in each square. The first theme is the "Unfinished" Symphony by Schubert which is No. 11, therefore, number eleven has been placed in the square.

1. "Surprise" Symphony (Haydn)
2. "Clock" Symphony (Haydn)
3. "Farewell" Symphony (Haydn)
4. Symphony No. 39 (Mozart)
5. Symphony No. 40 (Mozart)
6. "Jupiter" Symphony (Mozart)
7. "Eroica" Symphony (Beethoven)
8. Fifth Symphony (Beethoven)
9. "Pastorale" Symphony (Beethoven)
10. Seventh Symphony (Beethoven)
11. "Unfinished" Symphony (Schubert)
12. "Italian" Symphony (Mendelssohn)
13. Fourth Symphony (Schumann)
14. Symphony in D Minor (Franck)
15. First Symphony (Brahms)
16. Fourth Symphony (Tchaikowsky)
17. Fifth Symphony (Tchaikowsky)
18. "Pathetique" Symphony (Tchaikowsky)
19. "New World" Symphony (Dvorak)
20. Fourth Symphony (Mahler)

Teachers' Note: This game provides excellent ear training opportunity. Play the themes for the student and have him/her identify them. The game also can be adapted to provide entertaining instruction for music clubs and recitals.